The Art of Being Persistent: Overcoming to Become More

CRAIG A MORRISEY

Copyright © 2020 Craig A Morrisey

All rights reserved.

ISBN: 978-0-578-71309-0

Acknowledgements

WOW! This has been a journey. I'm incredibly grateful and thankful to God for giving me the insight and fortitude to be able to write this book. I must say, this book has been my most challenging one to write to this date. Everything dealing with *The Art of Being Persistent* pushed me and challenged me to see if I would stand on the principles God has giving me to give to the world. I'm honored God chose me to be a mouthpiece in this time and space to encourage and push others to overcome and become more.

As I reflect over the time it took me to write this book, I realize you always need special people in your life to push you and encourage you to not quit; and that person for me is my lovely wife. Crystal, I'm forever and deeply indebted to you for your love, encouragement, your push, and your undoubting faith in me to not let me give up when I was frustrated with writer's block. Your belief in me caused me to persevere and block out the noise to write like never before. I am forever grateful for you. I hope I made you proud that I was your husband because of my ***Persistent*** fight to finish what I started in writing this book. My love for you during this process has grown to a level I didn't know I had in me. Always remember, you have my heart! Thank you for being my sounding board in a time when I really needed it. I love you forever!

I would like to thank my parents, Loreta Jones and James Morrisey. To my mom, thank you for instilling in me hard work and dedication at an early age. I've watched you all my life beat the odds and overcome everything. It's because of you I know what it means to persevere, hold on, and keep the faith. To my dad, I'm grateful that our relationship has grown stronger over the years.

God has shown me a new bond and love between us and I'm thankful for it. I hope I make you proud to call me your son. To the rest of my family, I simply say, "Thank you!" I've never forgotten who raised me and where I'm from. That's because of the pride you instilled in me to be proud of my hometown and upbringing. I'm proud to say I'm from Warsaw, NC.

To my church family, thank you! To the greatest bishop in the world, Bishop Donald Crooms Sr, thank you! You took me under your wings back in 2003 and I've been growing ever since. I'm proud to say I'm a better man, husband, son, friend, servant, and leader because of your teachings and fatherly advice. Thank you for not holding back on me and pushing me to become everything God has locked on the inside of me. I'm still growing and have a hunger to know God more, and that is because of you. I don't know where I would be if destiny didn't align me with you and your ministry. Faith Tabernacle of Praise, I'm forever grateful for your love and support. I pray my success in life makes you proud of me and know that you all had a part in me becoming the man I am now. Also the man I inspire to become in the future.

Thank you to everyone who had a hand in helping me edit and design this book. Thank you for your hard work and years of experience. I don't take it for granted. Hopefully we build a partnership, which lasts into the future.

To the readers of this book, thank you! Thank you for trusting me enough to hear what I have to say. Thank you for allowing the words God gave me to help you and push you to become more. My prayer is this book inspires you and jump-starts your journey to live life in abundance; in every area of your life. I'm excited for you to experience what I've experienced as I wrote this book. How *Persistent* hard work and dedication allows us to obtain goals, dreams, and aspirations we've always had but were too afraid to go after them. Let's take this journey together in discovering *The Art of Being Persistent*!

Foreword

Morrisey's book *The Art of Being Persistent: Overcoming to Become More* is an inspiring, practical and fundamental tool for readers who have felt like throwing in the towel. Craig Morrisey pens a phenomenal work that speaks to the hurt of those who aspire to do more and to become more. The book pushes the reader into a "hungry and thirsty" and to discover a place of overcoming faith. The great author and poet, Maya Angelou stated, "There is no greater agony than bearing an untold story inside you". Morrisey breaks through the agony a bears a story inside of him that derives from experiences, challenges and victories.

The author at the end of each chapter using a thematic term "decree" to drop spiritual nuggets to not only read but to vocally speak positive, living words. Yes, our words have life and we can create a preferred world by speaking the Word of God. Morrisey is a true worshipper and it does not surprise me that he entitles a chapter, "Persistent Worship". He has been a musician for more than twenty-five years and has learned how to tap into the heart of worship. Man was created to worship and when he worships God, this positions him to be in alignment with the will of God for his life.

I have been pastoring for more than thirty years and I will admit there are times in life that it is difficult to remain persistent. Difficulties and challenges provoke a renewed attitude of persistence, especially when what you have hoped for and believed for is on the line. Morrisey's book will definitely speak to the leader, reader and Christian who have contemplated quitting. This is a must read and I believe it reveals the very heart of God for every believer.

    Bishop Donald Crooms Sr.

CONTENTS

	Introduction	i
1	Persistent Faith	1
2	Persistent Worship	Pg. 10
3	Persistent Love	Pg. 19
4	Persistent Obedience	Pg. 28
5	Persistent Pursuit Of Purpose	Pg. 37
6	Persistent Patience, Persistently Waiting	Pg. 46
7	God's Persistent Love Towards Us	Pg. 56
8	Persistent Pursuit Of God's Presence	Pg. 66
9	Persistent Personal Growth	Pg. 79
10	Persistent Happiness & Gratitude	Pg. 91
11	In Conclusion	Pg. 108

Introduction

Life has a way of introducing us to many different circumstances, challenges, and opportunities. In anything, it's what we do with those circumstances and challenges that create beautiful opportunities in life. While I sit here today writing this book, I'm reminded how this has been one of the hardest things I embarked on doing in my life. Not because I don't understand writing or know how to type, but because the process for this book has been a long one. The ebb and flow of trying to figure out how I wanted to start, or my thoughts for this book became overwhelming. I hit a wall in my preparation for writing, and it took me over a year to understand and put into words what I wanted to say to the reader. It was at that moment that I realized what the word **Persistent** meant.

As people often express, the light bulb went off in my head. I experienced the "eureka effect," better known as the Aha! Moment. I understood the thing I wanted to write about, I was experiencing firsthand. To not quit or succumb to the feeling of helplessness, I needed to be persistent in my pursuit of writing this book. Not just writing any book, but a book that would help people overcome challenges in life and also becoming *more* in every area of their lives.

One thing that puzzles me in writing this

book, is we often hear people tell us that they have to be consistent in their daily walk and catch the rhythm of this thing we call life. Don't get me wrong, there has to be a level of consistency in our daily routine, but we also need to have an unction to keep going when difficult moments present themselves to us. There is a beautiful opportunity awaiting us on the other side of the stumbling blocks in life.

To reach our full potential and become the thing we've been destined to become, we need to discover the *Art of Being Persistent*. As we embark this journey together, it is my prayer that we discover what it takes to become more and fulfill our purpose of what we were placed on this Earth to do. From this day forward, we will be persistent in our pursuit of life. Everyday we wake up we will face what life presents us and overcome it like never before. Our persistent drive to become better and live life on purpose will outweigh the difficulties life reveals at every turn. As the pages begin to turn, let's embark on this journey together as we explore *The Art of Being Persistent.*

Persistent Faith

"Don't abandon your promise because of your process. Allow yourself to develop fully and reap the benefits of your faith and perseverance."

Dictionary defines persistent as continuing firmly or obstinately in a course of action in spite of difficulty or opposition. When we awake everyday, we are presented with a couple of options—we can lie in bed and sulk, get up but not live, or we can face it head-on no matter the circumstances. As you can see, we have free will to do either one. Everything starts with a choice and an action. Our work ethic, steadfastness, and belief system has to line up in order for us to conquer our day ... and it starts with our faith.

The bible tells us in Hebrews 11:1, *"**Now faith is confidence in what we hope for and assurance about what we do not see.**"* Dictionary defines faith as complete trust or confidence in someone or something; also a strong belief in God or in the doctrines of a religion, based on spiritual apprehension rather than proof. What happens when our circumstances contradict our faith and cause us to lose sight of our goals and vision? How do we navigate through life's obstacle course when it seems we are stuck in a matrix of repeated cycles? I believe we need to have persistent faith that allows us to stand firm and trust beyond a shadow of doubt that our goals and vision will come to pass.

I began to study some successful people over the years, and realized they had a couple of things in common. For starters, they all have failed at one point in their lives. They all arrived at a roadblock in their careers or lives where they had to make a decision to find another route to take or give up. However, they didn't allow their failures to hinder them or their pride to stand in the way because people saw their failure.

Never allow people to make you feel embarrassed because of the detours in your life on your way to your promise. It actually shows your character, faith, and fortitude when you persistently pursue your destiny in the face of opposition. Detours never stop you from arriving at your destination. It's when you quit believing, and give up because the roads in your life are closed, that stops you from getting there. Even though it may take you longer, I would prefer you follow the detour and arrive, rather than quit and never reach your appointed destination.

As you know by now, it doesn't matter who we are in life, we all at some point will have to use our own measure of faith to get past obstacles and achieve our goals. It's our fundamental belief system that drives and pushes us, while we are in the process, to maximize every opportunity we have to get better everyday. It takes persistent faith to fall in love with the process when everything around us paints a picture that we should stop and throw in the towel. No matter what different variations the obstacles present themselves — whether sickness, finances, family problems, career, your goals, your dreams, or any other host of situations — there's always a process that takes place that we have to follow. Don't abandon your promise because of your process. Allow yourself to develop fully and reap the benefits of your faith and perseverance.

In our spare time, my wife and I love to watch the television show called *Chopped*. One thing that irritates the judges is when the food presentation is immaculate but the inside of the food is not cooked properly. The chef had a process they were supposed to follow, but it was cut short for one reason or another. At that very moment, the chef realized it was a grave mistake not to allow themselves to see it through to the very end. What looked ready to eat would have caused someone else to become sick.

When we abandon our process in life, we present ourselves as finished products with no substance on the inside. Your effectiveness to fulfill your assignment in life is crippled because of your inability to stick it out and see it through. Our lives should never be about what we get out of it alone. We should always strive to become more in order to better those around us and those we were put here on this Earth to help.

So you see, how we go through life has a lasting affect on everyone. There are many people watching you and following your lead whether you know it or not. I implore you to use your faith, press through and see your dreams, visions, goals, healing, and other things take place. Your persistent faith will empower you to touch a generation and show them the power of trusting and believing when you should give up. There is nothing more powerful than being able to look back at what you overcame to become everything you desired to be.

Today is the start of a new day for you. It is the day you decide to stick it out. The day you decree that nothing will keep you from your destiny or promise. Not sickness, depression, finances, hurt, roadblocks, forks in the road, family, friends, or etc. Now is the time you pick your dreams back up and run forward. Furthermore, you decide to use your persistent faith and become more of what God has called you to be in every area of your life.

Decree

Say this with me: *"I will be everything God called me to be. I will accept the challenge and move forward because the everlasting God has my back and fights for me. This is the day I pick up the thing that I gave up, put aside, or put on the back burner. From this day forward, my faith will help me move mountains and cause me to walk head-on into my Destiny. This is my Decree."*

Persistent Worship

"When you persistently and consistently worship God, you create an atmosphere in your home, family, and surrounding areas, which allows God to have permanent residence."

One thing I've found out over the years is life has a way of speeding us up if we let it. The world moves so fast, we spend most of it trying to assure when we arise in the morning, we have our whole day planned out. If you have children, you make certain they're up in the morning, getting ready for school, having breakfast, and either off on the bus or you're rushing out the door attempting to get them to school. Before that, you're trying to get yourself together a lot of times we feel rushed, and the day goes as such. We try to keep our daily routine because we believe that's what keeps us sane.

Before we realize it, we are back home, maybe preparing dinner, trying to see how everyone's day has gone so far or struggling to decompress from the long workday. Oftentimes, we bring work home with us, and everything else falls in place where it can. Before we know it, it's time for bed and we are off to do it again the next day. I have a question? Did we make space for God in our daily routine or did we do Him like we did everything else that day? Did we say He has to fall in place somewhere because my life is so busy? We use the excuse of "I just don't have time" and that's were we get ourselves in trouble. We attempt to encounter the day without his presence or direction.

I believe sometimes we have a misconception of what worship really is. For so many years, we've labeled it a certain thing, and it causes us to believe if we don't do it a particular way, we haven't really worshipped at all. So let's explore what worship truly is. Webster defines worship as a reverence offered a divine being or supernatural power, also an act of expressing such reverence. It also states that it is extravagant respect or admiration for or devotion to an object of esteem worship. Then we see that word reverence mentioned, and it has an important meaning. Webster states that it means honor or respect felt or shown: deference; a gesture of respect. So you see, everything we do should be as worship unto the Lord. Our lives should represent Him in everyway. One thing that helps us honor and revere Him in everything we do is spending time with Him.

David said in Psalm 63: ***"O God, thou art my God; early will I seek thee: my soul thirst for thee, my flesh longeth for thee in a dry and thirsty land, where no water is."*** David realized he had to be persistent in order to make God his priority. We need to have the same persistency to make sure we start our day out with God. Our lives get so bogged down with everything we have to accomplish throughout the day that it becomes a press to spend time with God.

I've come to realize when we prioritize time with God in the morning, it makes the day easier to handle. Believe me, I know it's a fight just to get out of bed some mornings. I understand what you have to do throughout the day is very important and it needs your undivided attention, but if I may pose a question … what about the one who breathes life into you every morning? How much of your attention does He have? Does God need to set an appointment with you to break into your busy schedule? Or do you go throughout the day and allow Him to wait on the backend?

Listen, I know what it's like to have to push myself and make sure I start my day off with Him. It is a persistent drive we need to have in order to make Him priority number one. One thing I love about my time with God is it's not a designated time period or programmed schedule. It's spontaneous worship toward Him. I'm not saying be late for work in the morning. I'm telling you that if you have to wake up ten minutes earlier, or however much time you need in order to spend time with God, do it. Your persistent worship toward God tells Him no matter what you have on your agenda for today, making sure He knows He's priority number one in your life is what you long to do.

It's at this place in your life you begin to persistently and consistently create an atmosphere in your home, family, and surrounding areas, which allows God to have permanent residence. When you allow God to have permanent residence, His glory, protection, love, peace, and joy allows you to walk in such a peace in your life that it puts you at ease. One of the greatest feelings in the world is knowing you are allowed to have God's presence in your life. This doesn't guarantee you won't face any trials, but it does ensure God is there when you face them.

Your worship toward God creates a place of honor and space for Him. When we're persistent in our worship, we show God reverence and the utmost respect. Our persistent worship helps keep Jesus at the center of our lives, and if we want to live this life to its maximum potential, keeping Jesus at the center remains our best possible solution.

Decree

Say this with me: *"From this day forward, my worship and lifestyle toward God will no longer be determined by the way I feel. My persistent worship toward God will always be predicated by who He is. My reverence toward God will allow me to live life on purpose. My worship will always create a space in my life for God to dwell, and the peace of God will always abide in my life. This is myDecree."*

Persistent Love

"Your persistence to love outweighs circumstances, trials, hang-ups, and disappointments."

As we continue to grow as a society, there's one thing not shown enough of in this world and that is love. It seems sometimes there's a "but" or negative connotation after love statements. It makes me wonder how much better would this world be if we genuinely showed love to one another? What changes would occur around the world? How much better would our lives be? Would our families look different? Would relationships work better because the love is real and put into action; not just lip service?

Also, we have to ask ourselves some hard questions. Are we the problem? Do we show love? Is our love genuine or is it contingent upon different circumstances? Most importantly, do we love ourselves? When we as a society can start answering these questions, I believe we will begin loving in a way like never before. One thing I want to start a dialogue about; do we love ourselves?

In the book of Matthew, the 22nd chapter, verses thirty-six through thirty-nine, we see God giving the two greatest commandments of the law. First, Jesus says, **"Thou shalt love the Lord thy God with all thy heart, and with all thy soul and with all thy mind."** This is the first and great commandment. Jesus then makes the second greatest commandment to us all, which is, **"Thou shalt love thy neighbor as thyself."** As we can see, both of these commandments contain a common action word—*love*.

Let's focus on the second commandment for a moment. Love thy neighbor as thyself. Studying the world today, this commandment is lacking and there is a glaring reason why. One phrase in the second commandment says as thyself, but what I see today in the world, people have allowed society, social media, and different avenues to determine their self-worth. Their self-worth is affected by the highlights of people's lives rather than what God has put on the inside of them and what God has blessed them with. When I say blessed them with, that's not material things, it is their own uniqueness and likeness. How can you love your neighbor, family, friends, and loved ones when you not only don't love yourself, but also don't even like yourself?

With the pressure the world puts on people trying to look like this and be like that, we need to be persistent and fight to love ourselves for who we are. Studies have shown that when you love yourself, it breeds confidence in yourself. When you have confidence in yourself and are comfortable being you, it's easier to love someone else. You're not jealous or envious of people because of their looks. You're able to celebrate others and show genuine appreciation. So if we're honest, loving people has a lot to do with how we see ourselves.

One thing I want you to understand, I'm not telling you not to work on yourself, as far as if you want to lose weight or something to that extent. I'm simply stating don't let your deciding factor to work on yourself be to look like someone else to determine your self-worth. Be who God designed you to be, there is no one else in the world that can pull off being you. Even people who are identical twins have their own uniqueness and purpose. In their identical likeness, their fingerprints or the number of strands of hair on their head aren't the same. As the reader, I want to encourage you to fall in love with *you* all over again. Be persistent in your love for yourself. Know your self-worth, and watch how you begin to treat others for the better.

Since we've dealt with loving ourselves, I want us to focus on the action behind the word "*love*". If we are completely honest, it takes work to truly love. I believe we take the word love too loosely. The dictionary defines love as an intense feeling of deep affection; also a great interest and pleasure in something. Let's focus on the first definition. It says intense feeling of deep affection. The word intense is not a word to be taken lightly. The word intense means: of extreme force, degree or strength. It's also having or showing feelings or opinions. Most of the time when someone uses the word intense to describe something, they are trying to let you know they have immense passion about what they are doing. This is the way we should feel when we use the word love. There should be a great passion behind it. It also should move you from not just lip service, but putting your love into action.

There should be a persistent pursuit to love

the way the word is intended to be used in our vocabulary. In our relationships, marriages, family, and society, we should be striving every day to make the word *"love"* come alive by our actions. I believe wholeheartedly when we, as a world, began to stop taking this word lightly, we will see positive change everywhere. I'm not saying everything will be easy, but when you *love* someone, you are willing to fight to make things work. You are not easily persuaded to quit or give in. Your persistence to love outweighs circumstances, trials, hang-ups, and disappointments. Love conquers all, and when we remember how powerful love is, things will always work themselves out for the better. So today, let's make a decree to love the way we should love.

Decree

Say this with me: *"From this day forward, I will never use or take the word love lightly. I will focus my energy to love with passion. My love will change not only my surroundings, but also everyone that comes in contact with me. No matter if it's my marriage, family, relationships, or friends, my love will persistently and passionately pursue avenues to make things better. Today, I will stand by the phrase 'Love conquers all'. This is my Decree."*

Persistent Obedience

"There are many different ways to honor and worship God, but I've come to realize, obedience is the highest form of worship there is."

As I sat here and thought about the world today, I began to wonder one thing: Do we really trust God? I mean, we say we do, but when chaos, trials, circumstances, or turmoil happens, what is normally our first point of action? Do we draw close to God or do we feel as if God has left us here to deal with things on our own? As I reflected on my life, it was a process to begin to trust God. When we are young, we depend on our parents or guardians to be our provider and protector, but while we mature, it's our responsibility to build a relationship with God for ourselves. The greatest way to show God that you trust Him is your obedience.

There are many different ways to honor and worship God, but I've come to realize, obedience is the highest form of worship there is. We show God the ultimate form of respect when we obey Him. It takes us letting go of our will and submitting to the will of our Father in Heaven.

And believe me, I know it's not an easy thing all the time. There are many instances in my life I wanted to do my own thing or make a decision where I thought it was best for my family or me but it wasn't in the will of God. It was in that space of time, I had to ask myself a question. Do I follow God or do I do what I think is best?

The bible has many scriptures that deal with these same scenarios. Proverbs 16:9 says, *"**We can make our plans, but the Lord determines our steps.**"* Also, Proverbs 14:12 says, *"**There is a way that appears to be right, but in the end it leads to death.**"* Another one is Proverbs 3:5, which states, *"**Trust in the Lord with all your heart and lean not on your own understanding.**"* As I began to study God's word, I quickly started to see, when we trust our own judgment, we are subject to mess it up.

What I love about God is He gives us free will to do as we please. God presents us with instructions and leaves the rest up to us. It's then, at that very moment, our obedience is tested. We bring God joy when we understand our ways and plans do not compare to God's plans for us. God tells us in Isaiah 55:8, *"For my thoughts are not your thoughts, neither are your ways my ways."*

One of the many reasons I love God, He doesn't stop there, explaining to us why it's best to obey and trust his plans and direction. God tells us in Jeremiah 29:11, *"For I know the plans I have*

for you, declares the Lord, plans to prosper you and not to harm you, plans to give you hope and a future." So, you see, our obedience to God saves, protects, and blesses us all at the same time.

Now, listen, it takes work to be able to obey God at all costs. I would never tell you it is easy, and when you hear God's voice you just automatically start doing everything He says the first time. As is in any relationship, the more you get to know God, you understand who He is. Then you begin to trust His Word. This is not just a one-way street. Your persistent obedience to God allows Him to trust you. This is a great place to be in. When God trusts us, He reveals Himself to us like never before. He begins to talk to us and show us things we could never dream or imagine. It's then our relationship becomes like Adam and God, where he searches us out just to have a conversation. It brings Him joy to know He has your ear.

Now I must warn you, obedience sometimes leaves you looking a little crazy. Obedience is occasionally a walk by yourself. Not everyone is willing to obey God at all costs. So your obedience can never be predicated upon someone else's judgment or willingness to follow God's instructions. Not everyone is willing to sacrifice their lifestyle and plans for their lives. This type of obedience takes sacrifice and you have to fight to do it. You need to be persistent. You have to stand strong, and know that God has your back. And if he said it, you will obey and trust Him no matter what.

This type of obedience has to become your lifestyle. When we are able to have this level obedience in our lives, our hearts are open to God in ways we wouldn't believe. It's no longer what we want in life that matters. It becomes, "God, whatever you want out of me, I will do. Whatever your plan is, I'm all in."

When we reach this place, life, as we know it changes. So I implore you today, begin to learn God for yourself. Develop a relationship with Him that goes beyond His hand. Seek his face. Just know the closer you get to God, the more He requires out of you.

Are you willing to obey at all costs? God is waiting on you. Let today be the day your obedience moves you past what you can see to what you hear from God. Because when you obey from His word alone, what you can see becomes endless and limitless.

Decree

Say this with me: *"Father, today I make the necessary steps to get to know you better. In doing so, my relationship with you will cause my obedience to grow to another level. And it is at this place in my life, I will follow you at all costs. So I vow to you today, with the help of the Holy Spirit, my obedience will become my highest form of worship to you. I love and trust you always. This is my Decree."*

Persistent Pursuit of Purpose

"There is a peace, which sustains us when we are walking toward purpose and destiny."

As I began to think about some past events in my life, I was reminded of a sermon I preached,

"Your Purpose is Greater Than Your Pain". I talked about the pain that life offers you, while you're on your way to discovering your purpose and destiny. After I finished, one of my mentors approached me, congratulated me, and told me he was proud of me. Then the next few words he spoke to me stuck out above everything else spoken to me that night.

He said, "You do realize you are going to be tried in your life to see if you will push past your pain to get to your destiny, right?"

It was if I was given a public service announcement. Those words have been my motivation to push past every circumstance I've encountered so far in my life.

Now, I'm not telling you it has been easy to push past those circumstances; it took some persistence, faith, dedication, and determination to believe what God has spoken over my life. Sometimes, there were days it seemed as if it was a constant battle to believe or not. Those are the times you must encourage yourself and keep positive motivation around you at all costs. Your life depends on it. Not just your life, the people who are connected to you depend on it.

I believe when we see the bigger picture outside of ourselves we begin to see purpose at its highest potential. Our life should never be about me, me, and me. Just about every CEO of a company, who has been successful, created a product thinking about the consumers. Well we should have the same thought process when we operate in our purpose. Our purpose should always have an impact on our family, communities, and the world. If our purpose doesn't operate like that, we need to do some self-evaluation.

We should be asking ourselves tough questions like, "Why do I want to be successful? What impact will my purpose have on everyone connected to me? Are my goals purpose-driven or are they full of selfish ambition?"

When we can answer those questions truthfully, we are on the way to pursuing purpose at all costs.

A critical reason why you should always be in persistent pursuit of your purpose is it rejuvenates your passion to live life to the fullest everyday. One of the worst feelings in the world is when you wake up and have no desire to accomplish tasks in your day. You would rather lie in bed or stay home instead of fulfilling your assignment. I've been around people who go through life with an attitude of barely getting by, and if it happens it happens. Those types of attitudes are contagious if you are not careful. You will find yourself complaining more than being grateful for another day to find the answers in which we are seeking. It should be a persistent pursuit everyday to surround yourself with positive people and positive affirmations.

Now, I'm not telling you to totally distance

yourself from people. You might be the very person they need in order to become what God has called them to be. I'm telling you we have to be mindful of our time. There is no need to keep investing yourself into someone if they have no desire to become better or change. When we are persistent in our pursuit of purpose, we have to make hard decisions in life to see if people are sponges or leeches. A sponge soaks up everything you pour out and tries to hold it all in to the best of their capabilities. A leech attaches itself to you in order to suck the life out of you and causes you to move at a slower pace. When we can determine the difference between the two at an early stage in our relationships, we save ourselves headaches and our own manufactured stumbling blocks.

While we are maneuvering through life, people, and circumstances, purpose should always be the driving force to propel us to achieve our goals and destiny. There is a peace, which sustains us when we are walking toward purpose and destiny. The peace comes about when we know we are on the right track in life. I stated in a chapter before, never allow setbacks to discourage you to the point of quitting. Reassess your strategy, formulate a new plan, and pursue purpose once again.

I believe in you, and I know you can achieve everything God has spoken over your life. Your purpose is waiting on you. It's up to you to reach your full potential. What's it going to be? Will you make up in your mind today that no matter the obstacles you'll pursue your purpose? Or will you allow life to keep you stagnant and afraid to live an abundant life? I implore you today to choose your purpose and destiny. The world will be better off if you do!

Decree

Say this with me: *"Today I make the decision to persistently pursue my purpose like never before. This will be the last day I allow my circumstances, obstacles, life, and people to hinder me from achieving the abundant life God has designed for me. My purpose will initiate positive change in my life, family, community, and the world. Life, as I know it, is changing for the better, because my persistent pursuit of purpose is rejuvenating and strengthening me to reach for new heights in my life. I will walk in purpose, and my faith is colliding with my actions to produce my destiny. This is my Decree!"*

Persistent Patience

Patiently Waiting

"We've become so dependent on the statement, 'We are waiting on God', that we are literally sitting idly by, doing nothing and allowing time to waste away."

I began to study some of the biggest corporations in the world; I noticed a lot of them had some key things in common. One of the key things I found in a lot of their success stories was things don't happen overnight. It was a process and it took an unbelievable amount of patience while waiting for things to come together. Some of the most amazing companies that we see today started in garages, basements, bedrooms, or even their cars. It took determination and being persistent while they were patiently waiting for their dreams and goals to come to fruition. Could you imagine how vastly different the world would look today, if they would've quit because their dreams and goals didn't materialize as fast as they would've liked?

Some of the greatest inventions that we use

today took time to develop and be perfected. As I studied society, I realized one trait we lacked was the ability to patiently wait for things to develop and mature. Everyone seems to be in a rush to out-do each other in life. It has now become a world of who gets it out or accomplishes things first, no matter if it's wrong or inconsistent. We become so anxious and rush our dreams, relationships, business deals, marriages, inventions, projects, etc.

The process of waiting has somehow become synonymous with rejection and failure for some people. Meaning, if it hasn't happened in the timeframe we thought it should, we automatically perceive it wasn't our time or it wasn't meant to be.

Maybe it's something I need to come back to at a later date. Perhaps my dream was too big. Maybe it was not meant to be. These are the thoughts that permeate our minds, causing the feeling of failure. We have to fight them, and learn how to let patience work though us.

The ability to be persistent while patiently waiting is something we all should be striving for everyday. James 1:4 say, **"But let patience have its perfect work, that you may be perfect and complete, lacking nothing."** There is a misconception, which has us as a society believing that waiting means doing nothing. We've become so dependent on the statement, **"We are waiting on God"**, that we are literally sitting idly by, doing nothing and allowing time to waste away. That is not what that statement means. It means while we are waiting on God to breath on or manifest our dreams, we are persistently working toward our goals. We are allowing patience to mature us, strengthen us, and build character in us.

Our faith in God becomes so strong when our anxiousness doesn't cause us to quit. The perseverance in us becomes stronger when we allow patience to complete its work in us. Patience also causes us to lack nothing in every area of our lives. If we allow it to work the right way, patience will go through our lives like a fine-tooth comb. One thing I like about a fine-tooth comb is it gets everything at the root. We can use bigger combs to comb our hair to make it look decent in order for us to be presentable, but when we want our hair to look immaculate, we use fine-tooth combs to straighten out the roots.

Sometimes the process of using a fine-tooth comb hurts because we are straightening out things that are tangled up and matted together. We are separating things the naked eye can't see unless we inspect it in full detail. This is what patience does to us when we let it have its perfect work. It combs through our lives in detail, pushing out everything that's not like God. Sometimes the process hurts because we are giving things up that are not good for us. We are relinquishing our will to the Father's will. But I promise, if you allow patience to have free reign over your life, the timing of things coming to pass in your life will not have a stranglehold over you.

Your persistent drive to accomplish your dreams, visions, goals, relationships, marriage, and other things will fall into place at the correct time.

One thing we must understand, when we relinquish our will to the Father's will, our timeframe changes. We have all wrote things down in years past that we decreed would happen by this age in our lives. We wanted to have this by twenty, have that by thirty, this by forty, and so on. There is nothing wrong with having goals. We have to realize that our timing is not God's timing. So if things don't happen when we plan, we don't become distraught and feel like we have wasted time and energy. We have to continue to allow patience to have its perfect work over our life.

So remember, when patience matures in us, it's perfected and we lack nothing. I am not saying we won't have obstacles or delays. It's when those obstacles and delays arise in our life, our faith is not shaken. We understand persistent patience is working on our behalf to make us into the person God intended us to be. Our attitude is now changed from agitation to gratefulness because we know we are being groomed to walk in an abundant life full of endless possibilities because patience is perfected in us.

Decree

Say this with me: *"Today I decree over my life persistent patience in order to fulfill my purpose in this life. I will no longer rush myself or allow anxiousness to cause me to feel like a failure or rejected. From this day forward, patience will work its perfect work in me. Because I am relinquishing my will to the Father, my life will lack nothing. I will become everything God intended for me to become. Time will not defeat me. Time will not cause me to quit because my timing is not God's timing. So since my timing is not God's timing, I will put my faith and trust in God because He knows what's best for me. This is my Decree."*

God's Persistent Love Toward Us

"God's persistency and consistency to love us knows no limits. All He wants us to do is embrace His love."

Have you ever sat back and wondered, *God, why do you love me the way you do? After all I've done in my life, why do you still love me beyond measure?*

Those are the type of questions I ask God. I mean, if we're not self-righteous and prideful, we can admit God has had plenty of chances to not show His love toward us but He does it anyway. Maybe I'm speaking for myself here, but I can admit, everything I've done in my life hasn't always been what God has asked me to do. There have been some times I felt He should have given up on me. He should have washed His hands with me, but He didn't. Instead, His response was, "I'm going to love you harder and in excess." How many people do you know who would do that?

As you begin to study about God, there are

always words that are synonymous with his love. Forgiveness, goodness, mercy, grace, kindness, and compassion are some of the attributes of God in which it makes it impossible for Him to not love us. I'm sure we all can attest to some of these words being something we had to pray for or hope for from God.

Forgiveness is a word I ask for daily from God. I've learned that I'm never going to be perfect in my life. Everyday we all strive for excellence, but there are some things we fall short on. I'm thankful even in our shortcomings, God loves us all so much he offered His only Son up to be the sacrificial lamb for us. Even before we could disappoint Him, God put in a contingency plan for us.

Now if that's not love, I don't know what is. God displays a persistent type of love toward us that, if we're honest, sometimes family doesn't even show us. When we can look at God's love through the lens of forgiveness, it should always cause us to be eternally grateful. I'm pretty sure we all can take time, reflect, and think of things we know God should have kept His forgiveness. How many times have we asked for forgiveness and still ended up doing the same thing over again? Yet, God forgives us. How many people you know forgive you like that?

God's persistent love is stronger than anything we could ever dream of or imagine. First

Timothy 2:4 says that God wishes all men would be saved. Now, God knew everyone would not come to love Him and get to know Him on a personal level, but it was still His desire. The love He has toward humanity compels Him to hope beyond hope. Even though He knows the outcome of every situation, His persistent love for us causes for Him to hope even though some will never make the decision to love Him that way. This is the type of God we serve. Aren't you glad mercy and grace compel Him to love us this way? Could you imagine life without God's love for us?

I'm a person who loves to ask God questions. Even though I know sometimes He's probably thinking, *here he comes with those same questions again.* God sits there and listens to me over and over again; and I love that about Him. My questions are not so small to Him that I feel like He brushes me off or He doesn't have time for me. He wants us to be as little children coming to Him. If anyone knows children, it seems as if they can ask a million questions. Sometimes it will be the simplest thing, but to them, it's their whole world. If we are not careful, we, as adults or as a parent, will become frustrated because of the constant questions. Well, to God, that's music to His ears. He wants us to be inquisitive. When we're asking Him questions, He has our attention; and if He has our attention, we have His heart. When we have His heart, we have everything we need.

Now, I'm sure there are many ways God shows His love toward you. To you, it may not be forgiveness; it may be His grace, comfort, mercy, or more. No matter what way you feel God's love, just know God loves you more than you can ever comprehend. God gives us love in excess to make sure we know it. God's persistency and consistency to love us knows no limits. The word of God tells us in Romans 8:35: *"Who shall separate us from the love of Christ? Shall trouble or hardship or persecution or famine or nakedness or danger or sword?"* There are so many things listed in this scripture to let us know God is serious about His love toward us. There is nothing we can do to stop God from loving us. There's nothing that can happen in this world to draw His love away from us. All He wants us to do is embrace His love. Now, if you're reading this and you don't know God in this manner but you're feeling a tug on your heart to get to know Him this way, God's word has a simple solution. Romans 10:9 says, **"If you declare with your mouth, Jesus is Lord, and believe in your heart that God raised him from the dead, you will be saved."** See, it's really simple.

Pray this with me. *"God, I'm here answering your call. I'm thankful for your love and covering over my life even when I didn't deserve it. Please forgive me of my sins. I believe your son, Jesus Christ, died for my sins that I might have life in you abundantly. Come into my*

heart and change me for the better. I believe I am SAVED! " If you prayed that prayer and believed in your heart, I believe God has saved you. I'm thankful and overjoyed for you on your new walk in God.

Now remember, you're still not perfect. You're going to make some mistakes. But know now you have an advocate fighting for you. His name is Jesus Christ. So when God looks at you, He will see His son, Jesus Christ. The one who shed his blood on Calvary for us. That's our covering. Just know you have people around the world praying for you and cheering you on. You can do this! You can walk out this thing we call life because God is on your side.

Decree

Say this with me: *"Today I make the decision to allow God to love me. I will no longer allow my faults, hang-ups, disappointments, and other things to keep me from experiencing the persistent and constant love God has toward me. I ask God to forgive me for not allowing myself to grow close to him. For pushing Him away from me out of fear when He was drawing close to me. Today my life is going to be better because I will embrace God's love like never before. This is my Decree!"*

Persistent Pursuit of God's Presence

"I want an encounter with you like never before; and when I get in your presence, I don't want to leave."

As I look at us as a society today, there are

many things we are in constant pursuit of. We all have visions and goals we want to see accomplished in our lifetime before we walk away from this Earth. Those things keep us focused and our minds laser sharp. If we're really serious about seeing those things come to fruition, the determination on the inside of us never allows us to be stopped or deterred by any circumstances we might face. We sacrifice family time and other things in order to pursue our goals in life. Now could you imagine if we put the same effort and fervor into pursuing God? Not going after the things God can provide for us, but passionately seeking the face of God. I mean persistently pursuing God's presence at all costs. Could you imagine the encounter we would have with God?

The glory God would release on us all?

As humans, we should never try to equate the way we feel when it comes to how God would feel. Allow me to pique your curiosity for a moment ... How many times do you think people come to God in prayer just because He is God? Not asking for any blessings, but just want to genuinely spend time in God's presence because they miss Him? Don't get me wrong, I know it feels as if there is constantly something wrong and we always need a prayer to get answered. But how would you feel if every time someone came to you, it was because they needed money, help, or some form of blessing? Would you keep doing it with no questions asked, or would you eventually feel as if you are only needed when they need something? It's never just good, casual conversation, it's always I need this or that.

If we're honest, I believe we would become increasingly tired of a one-way conversation or relationship. We would feel as if we're being used. We would even start to duck or ignore them all together. How do you think God feels if every time we come to Him, it's always we need something?

Some may say, "He's God, so he understands what we need." That is a true statement, but could you imagine how God would feel if we started coming to Him in prayer? Saying, "Today, the only thing I want is your presence. I only want to seek your face and not your hand. I want an encounter with you like never before. And when I get in your presence, I don't want to leave." Could you imagine the feeling God would have when we put a premium on our one-on-one time with Him the same way we do with other things in our life?

As you're reading this, you may think I'm asking a lot of questions, and the truth is, I am. I want this chapter to be really thought provoking. I need us to examine our relationship with God as if we're looking through a magnifying glass. When we use a magnifying glass, the things we couldn't see before because they were so small become increasingly bigger. The fine print is no longer so small it isn't legible. We see things clearer than we ever have. This is what I want to happen when we dissect our relationship with God. I want us to have an honest conversation; a heart-to-heart type of conversation with ourselves. After this takes place, let's turn our focus back toward God.

As we begin to be honest with ourselves, it's very easy to become sidetracked by our petitions to God that we forget our reasonable service unto God. We become Romans 12:1, ***"Therefore, I urge you brothers and sisters, in view of God's mercy, to offer your bodies as a living sacrifice, holy and pleasing to God-this is your true and proper worship."*** This scripture tells us we should always be willing to worship God and revere Him with no hesitation. We shouldn't see it as a chore to spend time in God's presence. It should come as second nature to us to bask in His glory.

But today we are making a conscience effort to turn back to our first love. The same way God walked in the Garden of Eden in the cool of the day looking for Adam to talk to and fellowship with, we are going to meet God the same way. In Revelation 2:4, it says, *"Yet I hold this against you: you have forsaken the love you had at first."*

Do we remember how it was when we first accepted Christ in our lives? It was so refreshing to be able to talk with and spend time with God in His presence. We really didn't ask for things. We were so appreciative to God for allowing His only son to die on the cross for us. Which gave us permanent and free access to God. Even when we mess up, Jesus stands in front of us and shields us so God can soften the blow toward us. You remember that type of love, right? Let's get that love back and chase after God like we used to.

Now, as we begin to chase after God's presence, there are so many benefits, which naturally come to us. One benefit, which comes from God's presence, is a refreshing of our lives. When we enter into the presence of God, stress and worry can't follow us there. Our problems aren't allowed to chase us down into the presence of God. There is a sweet release that takes place in His presence. God strips us of doubt, cares of the world, relationship problems, and more. In those precious moments, nothing else matters. It's God and us alone.

Another thing, which takes place in God's presence, is change. Wherever God shows up, positive change must take place. There is nothing in your life, which isn't supposed to be there, that can stay when you are truly in the presence of God. God changes your environment. He changes your view on life when you're in His presence. Things, which would normally bother you, don't even faze you when you in His presence. After your encounter with God, your vision becomes clearer. The distractions in life may still be there, but because your vision is cleared up, you look totally past them.

It's as if God gives us an oil change when we're in His presence. One of the most vital parts in our vehicle is the engine. It's the heart of our car, truck, or SUV. After the engine runs for so long, the oil has to be changed out and new oil needs to be put in its place. Now, no matter how beautiful our vehicle is, if there is not oil in it, it cannot run. Matter of fact, if there is not enough oil in the vehicle, it could destroy the engine and we will have to spend thousands of dollars to replace it with a new one. When the mechanic changes our oil, all the dirty oil and debris that build up over time must be replaced with brand new oil. Or else our vehicle doesn't perform at its maximum potential.

It's the same way with us. As we go through life, we allow different types of debris to get into our system. It slows us down. We become ineffective. We're not producing fruit the way we should. The junk on the inside begins to shine on the outside. However, when we enter into the presence of God, the original mechanic begins to perform a spiritual oil change on us. Taking away the hurt, guilt, shame, defeat, disappointments, etc. God then replaces is with his love, peace, joy, happiness, gratefulness, and understanding.

As you can see, there are many benefits to seeking God's presence. Seeking His face. Matthew 6:33 tell us, ***"But seek first his kingdom and his righteousness and all these things will be*** *given to you as well."* We have a promise declared over us. When your first priority is God's presence, there is no good thing God will withhold from you. His love will always be with us and guide us where we need to go. I implore you today, go after His presence. You will never be disappointed when you do.

Decree

Say this with me: *"God, I'm sorry for not going after your presence the way I used to. I will never again allow my ambitions, goals, and dreams to occupy my time so much I forget about your presence. Today I make a vow to you. With your help, Father, I'm coming back to my first love. I'm rededicating my time back to you. I'm making it my personal goal to allow your presence to rest in my life forever and always. This is my Decree!"*

Persistent Personal Growth

"Complacency, procrastination, and always living in regret are the killers to persistent growth."

In my short time on this Earth, I've had the privilege of having different types of mentors to have an amazing impact on my life. The first true mentor to have an early impact on my life was my 4th grade teacher. Her name was Mrs. Angelina Smith. I can truly say, she was the first person to push me past what I thought I could learn. She never allowed me to shortcut myself. When I thought I was doing well, according to my standards, she always told me there's another level I could reach. I must admit, it was frustrating at times because I felt like she was nitpicking me. I always felt like she was singling me out in the class.

As I grew older, I started to understand why she pushed me the way she did. She saw beyond the 4th grader to which things came easy. She made me believe that learning was important and I should never stop learning no matter my age. Those days came in handy when I was in high school.

The next teacher, who had a profound impact on my life, was Mr. Jimmy Newkirk. He was everyone's favorite teacher in high school. Even though he was one of the hardest teachers, the way he cared for his students made you want to push yourself further. Now, as a junior and a senior, he taught English. Those were some of the hardest years of my life. I had to be persistent in learning things I never thought I could. The pressure he put on us to become better students ignited a fire on the inside of me for constant growth in different areas in my life. Still, to this day, some of his pet peeves and sayings are the driving force behind why I love writing and reading.

Another mentor in my life, who still is pushing me, is my pastor, Bishop Donald Crooms Sr. He is one of the few people I know who doesn't allow his age or whatever he's accomplished in life to deter him from learning more. That is inspiring to me. What it says to me is there is no excuse for me at my age to feel like I have arrived. His willingness to impart knowledge into my life and other's keeps me on my toes. Plus, he is the type of person to test you in ways you don't even realize you are being tested. I love that.

One, it makes me not be lazy, and two, I constantly have to yearn for knowledge and practical application.

Now, you may be asking, why are you going through listing these people in your life who are impacting you about knowledge? I'm glad you asked. You will always need people in your life to push you and help you accomplish things you never knew you could. No matter your age, degrees, or knowledge you knew before should ever stop you from persistently trying to grow. The world is always changing, and if we allow ourselves to become complacent with past accomplishments and old knowledge, we can become obsolete in our thinking and our ability to get the job done when needed.

I've seen so many people get replaced on jobs, and sometimes it had nothing to do with their age, but everything to do with their willingness to learn past what they already knew. The first thought in their mind is, 'Someone younger than me replaced me.' They immediately become defensive and begin to think they are being discriminated against. But the problem is, they refuse to learn new things. Technology is growing at a rapid pace, and if we refuse to learn, the next step is replacement. I love when I see stories of people in their 40's, 50's and 60's finishing college. They have put a premium on their brains learning and accomplishing more. Which should also say to us, the more we allow our brains to have activity, the more it keeps us alive and active. It's when we stop pursuing knowledge and growth we become stagnant, stale, and ineffective.

Not only should we persistently pursue knowledge, but also we should always strive for personal growth in every area of our lives. I believe we honor God when we strive to take care of ourselves and aim for wholeness as an individual.

Now listen when I say this: I know it is hard. A couple of years ago, started out with the goal to lose weight. Everything was going good until I hit a wall in my weight loss journey. For a while, I kept pushing and I wasn't seeing any results, not immediately. However, I slowly started to pull back on exercising, and allowed the good eating habits to fade away. Before I knew it, all the hard work I did for months was behind me and I had no results to show for it. I fell into a place of depression, and all the weight I lost, I gained back plus some.

One day, my wife sat me down and asked me, "What's something new you want to accomplish in your life?" I had many thoughts, but I knew I wanted to get back to my workout regime. She said, "We are going to do this together." However, I made the decision to say, "I'm going to do this for me." Now things are going slow and it's still a struggle sometimes. Especially during this pandemic—which is hitting our world hard—as gyms are closed, but my persistent will to become better is jump-starting my process to a better all around person.

So you see, I had to have a persistent determination to become a better individual. Falling down isn't failure. Failure is deciding to stay in that mindset. Your persistent fight in life may not be weight loss, but whatever it is, it will take persistence, fight, and determination to become better. I also surrounded myself with people who love me and want to see me better.

In your life, the people you surround yourself with determine your appetite to learn and grow. If your circle of friends are focused, have strong determination, are persistent fighters, and love to gain knowledge, you're more prone to have those traits rub off on you. We have all heard the saying, 'birds of a feather flock together.' Well, what do you think happens when you allow yourself to be pushed by those who constantly have a desire to become better everyday? Now, what happens when you allow yourself to be pulled by those who don't have a desire to get better?

See, it's up to us to decide which direction in life we take. We can allow ourselves to strive to be the best we can be in every area of our lives, or we can stay complacent and satisfied with mediocrity. Not only your life, but also the generations you have been called to reach depend on your willingness to grow. Complacency, procrastination, and always living in regret are the killers to persistent growth. Today, let's make the decision to become better. No matter the obstacles or roadblocks we may face, let our persistent willingness to grow become our strongest trait we display in this journey we call life.

Decree

Say this with me: *"Today is the day I make the conscience decision to become better in every area of my life. I will no longer allow obstacles and stumbling blocks to hinder me and cause me to quit. Failure is not failure when I fall. It's only failure when I don't get back up after falling. Today, I'm getting back up! I'm taking my life back. My persistent personal growth will be my fuel me to accomplish more in my life. This is my Decree!"*

Persistent Happiness & Gratitude

"The pain has purpose, and since it's necessary to walk in my destiny, I smile and make myself remain grateful."

As I'm finishing this book during a pandemic, one thing is for certain—you have to continually train your mind to be able to find the good even in the darkest of times. I'm learning you have to persistently pursue an attitude of gratitude even when you want to complain. Now, the easy thing would be to complain because, truth be told, we all can find reasons to complain. Every person in the world is inconvenienced in some sort of fashion. We are made to stay home and away from everyone. Some people can't work and things are not looking the very best at the moment. It's at these times we need to remind ourselves what we do have. We have to take inventory of what we're blessed with in spite of some crucial losses we may have experienced.

At our core, we are providers, protectors, leaders, and more. When things are taken away from us, which allow us to provide for our family and ourselves, it plays on our psyche. Our happiness tends to take a hit in the process. Some of us have had our happiness wrapped up into our careers, our status, and the way people perceive us. When we feel important, we allow it to determine happiness in the world. Well, when things are taken away, as during this pandemic, what do we have to fall back on? Do we still find things to help us remain happy and grateful, or do we allow every negative circumstance to dictate our actions?

Always remember during hardships, struggles, roadblocks, disappointments, etc., as difficult as it may be, we still control our level of happiness, joy, peace, and tranquility. God has given us some scriptures we can lean on. Philippians 4:8-9 says, *"Finally, brothers and sisters, whatever is true, whatever is noble, whatever is right, whatever is pure, whatever is lovely, whatever is admirable—if anything is excellent or praiseworthy—think about such things. Whatever you have learned or received or heard from me or seen in me—put it into practice. And the God of peace will be with you."* As we can see, we have a blueprint to follow even in our perilous times. We are told to think on things to remind of what God has done for us in the past and in the present. The scripture reminds us that even though we have a million things that can cloud our mind and judgment, don't give those things any thought. Our focus should be on what we do have and how blessed we are.

As you can see, the mind is a powerful thing. I'm sure we have heard the phrase 'you are what you think about and what you feed your mind.' Well, that is a true statement. There have been studies to determine what we give thought to have the power to seem real even if it's not. If we're not careful, our mind has the ability to make us paranoid, crazy, and hallucinate. But the same way our minds have the power for negativity, it has the power for positivity. It's up to us what we allow to conquer our thoughts.

As I stated before, we have a blueprint to

follow. Romans 12:2 says, *"Do not conform to the pattern of this world, but be transformed by the renewing of your mind. Then you will be able to test and approve what God's will is—his good, pleasing and perfect will."* This scripture has a lot we can follow. First, it says do not conform to the pattern of this world. The world's patterns are to become frustrated, agitated, and stay in a place of complaining. Now, I'm not saying you will never be frustrated or upset. Those are human emotions. But I am telling you not to make it your dwelling place. If we're not careful, it's easy to stay in a place of complaining. Everyday you wake up, there will always be something to complain about, but you must not wallow.

The next step in the scripture is key. It tells us to renew our mind daily. Meaning, we have to persistently feed our minds with things which Philippians 4:8 tells us to think on. Read good material to help create the thoughts we need to focus on. Study God's word and apply it daily. Even when your mind drifts and you daydream, remind it to get back inline with what God has said about you. Even what God has promised you! This causes persistent gratitude. Then your gratitude turns into happiness. Your happiness then produces joy, which causes you to gain strength in God's word.

The next part tells us after we have renewed our mind we will be able to test and approve what

God's will is. His good, pleasing, and perfect will. Now this part is very important because it gives us hope. You may ask how does it give us hope? I'm glad you asked. When we follow the steps of Romans 12:2, we can evaluate every circumstance we go through and see what can we learn out of it. We get to see how this situation aligns with God's perfect will for our life.

Over my lifetime, one thing I've found out about myself is, even though the circumstances may be dire and I feel like it would take me out, if it lines up with God's will for my life to bring me to what he's spoken over my life, I get a boost of energy. Even though it may hurt at the moment, I make my mind think about what God has said.

That he would never leave me or forsake me. The pain has purpose, and since it's necessary to walk in my destiny, I smile and make myself remain grateful.

So you see, we have to fight to make sure we are persistent in our gratitude and happiness. Another scripture, which gives us hope, is Romans 8:28. It says, *"And we know that in all things God works for the good of those who love him, who have been called according to his purpose."* We have a promise. No matter how bad it gets or no matter how big the obstacles are in life, *all* things work together for our good. Every situation we face has to come under subjection to our thought process; and that is, I will make myself continue to be thankful even in this. Why? Because all things are working for your good even when it doesn't feel good.

Which brings me to one of the most powerful things we have to fight against while persistently pursuing gratitude and happiness—emotions. Dictionary defines emotions as a natural, instinctive state of mind deriving from one's circumstances, mood, or relationships with others. Also it means instinctive or intuitive feeling as distinguished from reasoning or knowledge. One word inside of the definition of emotions is mood. As a society, this has become one of the new "it words". What I found out is our moods dictate our feelings and state of being. Not only that but our moods change like the wind. I've seen people go through different moods throughout the day, and to be honest, it looks exhausting. What we fail to realize is, if our moods change like the wind and with every circumstance, it overloads our mental capacity and makes it harder to combat the thoughts that are not of God for our life.

We have all heard the saying "Don't make difficult decisions when your emotions are running high". Because as humans, we tend to fly off the handle when we are not thinking clearly. These decisions lead to irrational thinking. Which determines how we see life. When our emotions get the best of us, we start to see life through the prism of our emotions. No matter how wrong our thinking may be, all we see is destruction and defeat. Well, this is no way to gain happiness and gratitude. This is actually the opposite of it. It will lead to walking through life thinking everyone else has it better and you will never get over the hump.

Your emotions aren't your compass. The word "God" is. The same can be said of toxic relationships. Sometimes we hold on to people when God is trying to separate them from us in order for you to walk in wholeness and happiness. As people, we are caring and helping at heart. We sometimes take on the responsibility of others when we shouldn't, and it's hard to relinquish them to God when he's trying to take the burden from us. Well, if we aren't careful, we take on their problems and circumstances. We tire ourselves out praying, believing, and fasting for them when they really only wanted to unload their problems and not change. We become fatigued, stressed, worried, and torn down because of carrying a burden not meant for us to carry. All of this has a tremendous affect on mental stability. It also effects our persistent pursuit of happiness and gratitude.

So if we don't guard our thoughts, fight against our emotions, and protect our sanity by watching our relationships, persistently pursuing happiness and gratitude becomes almost impossible. Regardless, I'm glad we have been given strategic plans to follow in order to help us conquer these things. When we follow the plans of God, even when life tries to knock us down, we have a promise that he will never leave us or forsake us. And to me, that's enough to be grateful for.

So remember, your happiness is not predicated on your circumstances. Your happiness shines through your circumstances and allows you to walk through life in a state of gratitude. Today, let happiness be your state of mind. As long as we live, life will always try to give us lemons when we are expecting apples and oranges. It's when we can take those lemons, squeeze them, sweeten them, and make us an awesome pitcher of lemonade that we start to take control of our life.

When you can take the sour moments of your life and see a better outcome, you're on your way to persistently pursuing happiness and living in a state of gratitude!

Decree

Say this with me: *"Today is the day I take back my happiness. I will no longer allow my circumstances to dictate my happiness and my gratitude toward God. I realize that no matter what I face, ALL things are working for my good. Everything that happens has a place and space in my life. But the joy of the Lord will always be my strength to overcome. I will renew my mind daily. I will remain steadfast in my thought process, which says God is going to get glory out of this. Today I command my mind to line up with God's perfect will for my life, because if it's his will for me, then I can take it and still be grateful. This is my Decree!"*

In Conclusion

As we transition to close this book, we find out there are many different things in life we should persistently strive to overcome. Our persistent drive to achieving a better life, not only for ourselves, but everyone connected to us should be on overload. There should be a tug on your heart to accomplish everything God has in store for you. The best way to walk in purpose is to make sure we are constantly checking our own selves. I believe we start to reach a level of maturity when we can look ourselves in the mirror and say some things need to change.

This is reaching a level of growth many never come to realize. It's not always the other person's fault. Sometimes, we are the problem. The sooner we start to realize it, the better life becomes for us. It's a dangerous thing to go through life thinking you have arrived. Thinking there is not another level God wants us to grow to. God loves us too much to allow our lives to be derailed by procrastination and complacency. What we fail to realize is, when we allow ourselves to become complacent, we tell God there is no more he can teach us. There are no more life lessons we can learn. We feel as if we have been enlightened and we have reached a stage of euphoria. This is a dangerous state of mind to live in.

One of the things I love about God is He loves us too much to not give us a way of navigating this life and overcoming obstacles. Even the obstacles we create for our own selves. God always has a plan we can follow in order to come out on top. Jeremiah 29:11 says, ***"For I know the plans I have for you, declares the Lord, plans to prosper you and not harm you, plans to give you hope and a future."*** This scripture relays to us, God is the master architect and he has the blueprint we should follow for the rest of our lives. His plans are our cheat code to navigate through life, our keys to persistently pursuing a better us.

Oftentimes we miss steps or get out of line in life because we stray away from the blueprint

God has designed for our lives. Before a contractor or builder can build a building, the architect has to design the blueprint. According to Webster, a blueprint is a photographic print in white on a bright blue ground or blue on a white ground used especially for copying maps, mechanical drawings, and architects' plans. Meaning it's a detailed plan or program of action. It's what the builder or contractor relies on to build. The architect has spent countless hours working over them to get them designed properly and make sure every fine detail has been raked through. They leave no stone unturned.

What people fail to realize is the blueprint is one of the most expensive things you need to buy when building. The reason it's expensive is because it is literally a bulletproof plan to come out with the best possible outcome from the foundation to the roof. Well, the chief architect of our lives, God himself, has laid out a bulletproof plan for us to follow. As we are the contractors for our life, it's up to us to follow the blueprint. Even when we hit some obstacles, we can't divert from the plan because his plan still works. It's only when we, as contractors, start to think we can do it on our own and build our own blueprint that we leave the will of God. This is a dangerous place to be when you are outside of the will of God for you life. His will for our lives are our failsafe.

Today, let's get back to following the

blueprint for our lives. God is so awesome because each one of us has our own blueprint drawn out. He created us to be special. My blueprint is not yours, and yours is not mine. Yours is not your neighbors' or friends'. So don't try to follow someone else's blueprint for your life. Each building that's ever been built has to be built with special modifications according to the area they are in. Meaning, when a building is built in a heavy storm area, such as near the water, there are proper steps and precautions that need to be taken that buildings or homes, which are on higher ground and not lower sea level, need to take.

Now just because those who don't live near the water don't have to take those additional precautions, it doesn't make the homes and buildings better or more desirable. Matter of fact, even though people know they have to take those steps to build a home or building near the water, they are willing to go the extra mile in order to secure their place on the water. The value of their property is usually higher because the area is more desirable. Meaning just because your blueprint causes you to do more to secure your foundation than others doesn't make you less desirable or behind. It means the area God has designed for you to walk in; you need to be able to withstand more; because he is placing a lot on your shoulders. Not everyone can handle those responsibilities.

So I pray this book has enlightened and

pushed you to strive for more. Not to draw back or say, "Whatever life presents me, I'm okay with it." God has so much more in store for us all. It's up to us if we are willing to persistently pursue God's goodness for our lives. Remember, God, our master architect, took his time to strategically design our blueprint for each of our lives. When we learn how to follow those plans and blueprints at all costs, no matter the price we have to pay, then we are on our way to maturity. It's at this place in life we start to discover *The Art of Being Persistent*.

My Prayer For You

God, I come to you on the behalf of this reader. First of all, Father, I want to tell you I love you. I'm so thankful for your love and kindness toward us all. You have been so good to us. There is no way we can thank you enough. I want to come to you on behalf of us and ask you to forgive our sins. We understand before we ask for anything, we need to make sure our hearts are pure. Secondly, I ask that you bless this reader. Allow them to find themselves in you like never before. I pray you won't let them settle in life. I pray you will take away their procrastination and complacency. I pray today, their drive to become all you have for them to be increases like never before. Today is the day their life changes for the better. I speak life into them and I decree everything you have spoken over their lives come to pass. On today, they will persistently pursue the greatness you design for them to live in. In Jesus' name, Amen!

Notes

THE ART OF BEING PERSISTENT

THE ART OF BEING PERSISTENT

THE ART OF BEING PERSISTENT

_____

_____

_____

_____

_____

_____

About Author

Craig Morrisey was born in Warsaw, NC, and now resides in Morehead City, NC. At a very young age, different gifts and leadership were instilled in him. He spent his years growing and striving to cultivate his gifts, talents, and relationship with God in order to help bless the world. He has always had a passion for people; striving to help them get closer to God while finding their purpose in life.

Craig obtained a Master's Degree in Theology and Biblical studies from North Carolina Theological Seminary in 2020. He's been the Minister of Music at Faith Tabernacle of Praise

International Ministries for fifteen years, where he strives to relay the message of the importance of having a relationship with God as a first priority beyond trying to perfect your gifts and talents. God has elevated him, and he is now an Elder Elect in line to become an Elder in the body of Christ. He travels to conduct various workshops and engagements to spread the message of persistent growth. It's his passion to see everyone grow in their relationship with God, themselves, and ministry.

He is the husband of Crystal Morrisey, whom he loves, adores, and has grown together with over fifteen years. Craig believes he wouldn't be where he is now if it wasn't for her love, support, and wisdom. He knows with God, family, and ministry, there needs to be a balance in your life. He believes, if you keep God the center of attention throughout your life, your drive and focus will continue to grow and build a foundation that changes this world to a better place.

References

Dictionary.com

King James Bible

NIV Bible

The Message Bible

Amplified Bible

Thesaurus.com

THE ART OF BEING PERSISTENT

www.ingramcontent.com/pod-product-compliance
Lightning Source LLC
Chambersburg PA
CBHW051944160426
43198CB00013B/2287